PEELING THE ONION

BRING YOUR RELATIONSHIPS BACK, LAYER BY LAYER

LEIGH BROWN

ILLUSTRATED by ZOE RANUCCI

Mallard Creek Publishing
PO BOX 396
Harrisburg, NC. 28075-0396

Limit of Liability/Disclaimer of Warranty:
While the publisher and author have used their best efforts in preparing this book, they make no representations or warranties with respect to the accuracy or completeness of the contents of this book and specifically disclaim any implied warranties of merchantability or fitness for a particular purpose. No warranty may be created or extended by sales representatives or written sales materials. Neither the publisher nor author shall be liable for any loss of profit or any other commercial damages, including but not limited to special, incidental, consequential, or other damages.

Library of Congress Number: 2020907238

ISBN: 978-1-943817-10-8 — softcover
978-1-943817-09-2 — ebook
978-1-943817-06-1 — audiobook

Ordering Information:
Quantity sales. Special discounts are available on quantity purchases by corporations, associations, and others. For details, contact the publisher at the address above or at **www.TheOnionBook.com**.

Printed in the United States of America.

DEDICATION

This is for you.
The one who always shows up.
The one who always has a hug.
The one who finds a way to elevate others.
The one who finds the light in the darkness.

I'm ever grateful to have crossed paths with you.

Contents

ACKNOWLEDGMENTS

Thank you to every online follower, liker, commenter, and viewer who has helped me create messages that matter. Your feedback guides me.

Thank you to everyone who has ever trusted me with their stage and their microphone. The gravity of that responsibility grows with each opportunity and with each attendee. I strive never to take it for granted.

Thank you to everyone who has ever entrusted me with their home sale or purchase. I know your options seem endless, so the trust is appreciated deeply.

Thank you to the support team I have locally. Your gifts and talents shine so brightly — I want so much to be YOUR support as you grow.

Thank you to Michele, Sandra, and Zoe for being the ones who made this book actually happen.

Thank you to Mama and Daddy, my aunts and uncles and cousins, and all those who have been with me since day one and would never abandon ship. I'm glad to have a shared history that is meaningful and growing.

Thank you, Cora and Tim. You absolutely take my breath away with your insights and humor and personalities. I'm so glad to be your Mama.

Thank you, Steve, for being willing to continue on this ride together.

Thank you, Jesus, for saving a wretch like me.

INTRODUCTION

Sometimes, it's a blessing to have things go off the rails.

Say, for example, this book. Which was *supposed* to be in your hands in 2019, yet it took a few months to navigate publisher waters. What happened in those few months?

Coronavirus, that's what. The shutdown of the world in light of a global pandemic, wherein many of us found ourselves in brand new situations, with brand new relationships and brand new ways of communicating.

I wrote this book in light of the desperate need many people are feeling — the need for connection — brought to its knees by the surface living of social media. As it turns out, Coronavirus could be the gift that gives us more than a sense of panic and fear — it could be the very reason we shed our desires for the perfect relationships and reality and get back to the humanity that truly matters.

From the daily hair/makeup/professional dress routine, during Coronavirus, many went to a routine of ballcap ILO hair/who needs makeup?/but these yoga pants are clean, with an understanding that this new normal affects most of us in some way. It's been freeing to hear people admit their economic fears — and have neighbors relieve them by helping. To hear people admit their fear of being an interim homeschool teacher — and have actual homeschool parents provide resources. To hear of people who crave a hug and a shared supper and who have now sworn NEVER to turn down a party invitation again!

How do we maintain this sense when the Coronavirus is nothing but the memories of empty toilet paper shelves? By peeling the onion, friends. Creating a healthy relationship that consists of the great and the awful. The grace which we should have offered anyway becoming a natural offering.

By getting back to where we all started as kids. Back to the sandbox where the games were better, when you shared the bulldozer, and throwing sand was shut down quickly. Walk through this journey with me and spend a little time in honesty with yourself so that you can spend that same time in honesty with your friends and neighbors.

It's possible. And the payoffs? *They are life-changing.*

Chapter 1.

What Happened to Us?

MySpace. Facebook. Twitter. LinkedIn. Instagram. Snapchat. And those are just the ones on my personal phone *(...okay, fine, I finally *did* delete MySpace!)*. It's everywhere, in all of our lives. To a one, we were excited when we signed up for our profiles and immediately launched out there looking for old friends and acquaintances and the guy who used to sit in the next cubicle and with whom you had lunch that one time.

Then it got old. Burdensome, even a bit depressing. Most people can point to the Presidential election of 2016 as the time when they finally lost patience with social media....and with friends and family who were proudly blocked and unfriended.

Proudly. As in, you removed people who you had previously enjoyed simply because of what they said online or because you now knew things with which you disagreed.

Now you find yourself wishing for the old school relationships in some degree but aren't sure what to do next — or who to trust — or what you can and can't say — feeling a little more lonely and depressed, as it turns out.

Peeling the onion means reconnecting with real people in the real world by getting to the heart of what is good and sweet, like the center of the onion. We can debate how much of a problem social media has become in our own lives, but statistically, it is a growing problem impacting the joy available to us in this life. I say it's time we resolve this and dedicate ourselves to living more fulfilling lives by stepping away from the computer and putting down the smartphone. As a side benefit, we might even reduce the wear and tear on our texting thumbs. There's also the potential for achieving greater happiness.

For me, it always begins with understanding the problem: what it is, where it came from, and how we got to today. With that in mind, let's take a look at an abbreviated history of social media.

Steve Jobs unveiled the iPhone to an adoring audience on June 29, 2007. Here was a device that allowed you to make calls just like any other cell phone, but it had a touch screen! Revolutionary! You could connect wirelessly to the Internet, play thousands of songs with your fingertips, get lost for hours in cartoonish games, and send text messages in an instant. One little glass and plastic rectangle took the place of 3, maybe 4 separate gadgets. You didn't need an iPod anymore. You no longer had to lug a laptop around. While traveling with little kids, if you forgot to pack their portable Nintendo or *(gasp)* a book, it wasn't the end of the world; they could play plenty of games on your phone. In other words, the iPhone was a massive hit. A tool that would fit just right with the ecosystem of social media *(still in its infancy, remember)*, the timing of the iPhone couldn't have been better. Twitter had launched just a year earlier. By the time Apple turned the iPhone loose, what we now know as Facebook had already been online three years but by 2007 was just starting to hit critical mass *(and deal with its first batch of privacy-related lawsuits)*. A year later, the first Android smartphone reached the market to compete with Apple's iPhone. By 2010, Facebook was a raging success, and probably everyone you knew had a touchscreen smartphone in their back pockets *(introducing new insightful vocabulary like the 'butt dial')*.

Three years after the introduction of the iPhone and an explosion of competitors, smartphone users more than doubled in the United States from 2010-2012, according to The Internet Innovation Alliance, a group of business and non-profit organizations. This year, the number of smartphone users in America is expected to reach nearly 249 million. That's more than 71 percent of the U.S. population and expected to climb to nearly 73 percent in the next two years. You realize that means a smartphone is chirping in 3 out of 4 American homes! It's no secret that those phones are attached to a hand most hours of the day *(including when you're showering or having sex — seriously, people)*.

Where Does the Time Go?
I'm amused and sometimes astonished when friends and acquaintances tell me they don't have the time to get everything done. No time to hit the gym, they complain. No time to meet someone for lunch or even just coffee. No time to participate in a book group or join a wine club. It seems like we're always out of time — complaining out how 'busy' we all are.

This would be troubling until you consider how much time we spend on social media. And how it just keeps on growing.

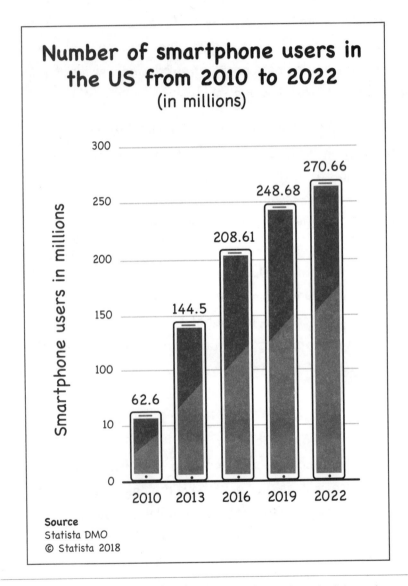

Number of smartphone users in the US from 2010 to 2022
(in millions)

Smartphone users in millions

- 2010: 62.6
- 2013: 144.5
- 2016: 208.61
- 2019: 248.68
- 2022: 270.66

Source
Statista DMO
© Statista 2018

Data Source: https://internetinnovation.org/general/research-peek-of-theweek-smartphone-users-in-the-us-expected-to-reach-over-270-million-by-2020

Young people ages 16-24 invest the most time on social media, about 3 hours a day, according to a study by Digital Information World *(honestly, I think this is a low estimate)*. If you're between the ages of 25 and 44, chances are you're spending an average of at least 2 hours a day on social media platforms that same study found. Middle age doesn't prevent people from frittering away more than 90 minutes a day on Facebook, Instagram, Twitter, and anywhere else they haunt online. Even the elderly manage to put in more than an hour every day on social media.

Daily time spent on social media
by age–hour:minute

If young adults actually realize they're squandering the equivalent of almost three full workdays every week on social media, they're not doing anything about it. If we take the U.S. average of 2 hours a day in 2018, that's 14 hours a week, which equals 728 hours over the course of a year. That's 30 days and 8 hours! My point is this: if you spend just the average amount of time on social media, it's consuming a MONTH of your life every year. No wonder nobody has time to do anything else!

Data Source: https://www.digitalinformationworld.com/2019/01/how-much-time-do-people-spend-social-media-infographic.html

So What's the Problem?

Social media is no substitute for human interaction. We are, by nature, social creatures. We're meant to talk to each other, sing together, laugh together and, yes, cry together. Social media robs us of that birthright. Too often, a sad-face emoji takes the place of a hug and a genuine conversation. Sure, it's easier to toss a little note of sympathy on Facebook when someone hits a rough spot in life, but what have you really accomplished? Band-Aids don't heal broken bones.

What's worse, social media creates a self-perpetuating cycle. People try to present the "perfect" image of themselves on their social media profiles and in everything they post. That image may not pass the reality test when they meet each other in person. So they don't. We'll get into this in greater detail later in the book.

I often turn to The Bible for comfort, for words of wisdom and inspiration. One day I got to thinking how the creation story might have turned out differently if the technology that consumes our lives today had been available during those ancient times described in the Old Testament.

Genesis 2 tells us Adam and Eve were brought together by God. They obviously didn't have social media to deal with, which was a lucky break for them. No awkward back-and-forth over the smartphone. No misunderstandings caused by the lack of context missing from text messages and emails and little emojis. Dare we imagine what texting might have been like thousands of years ago? Yes, let's.

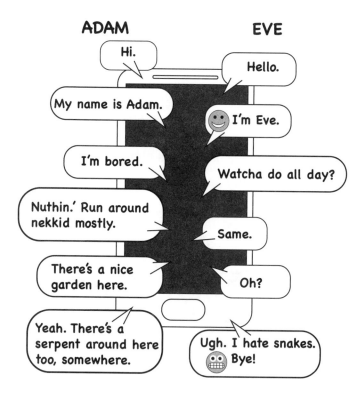

And so the human race would have ended before it began.

Yes, besides eating up our time, social media and technology have turned dating upside down. Some might even say social media has all but ruined dating. People use their social media profiles to present an idealized image without letting others see for themselves in the only way one individual truly gets to know another: in person. All the while, they're searching for someone who's got the perfect profile — and expecting it to be real! For some, meeting in person involves a risk they simply cannot overcome. That's because, well, no one is perfect, and it's terrifying to be found out. So they hide behind their profiles and another day goes by.

From the Garden of Eden, we fast-forward thousands of years to Tinder, which has people rejecting each other with a dismissive hand swipe based solely on surface characteristics. I find that incredibly sad. Yet this is where we are today. This is the challenge.

Overcoming that challenge is what we aim to accomplish by *Peeling the Onion*. As it happens, doing nothing could be bad for your health.

One Is the Loneliest Number That You'll Ever Do

We're more 'connected' than ever before. At the same time, many of us feel lonelier than ever before.

In 2018 the Kaiser Family Foundation produced an international study of loneliness and isolation. The organization found that 20 percent of Americans "always or often feel lonely or socially isolated, including many whose health, relationships, and work suffers as a result." Health. Relationships. Work. Can we agree that those are foundational to living happy, successful lives?

A majority of Americans surveyed (58%) see the increased use of technology as a major reason why people are lonely or socially isolated. In the U.K., 50% said technology and social media are to blame for the spike in loneliness.

Around the same time, the health insurance company Cigna surveyed 20,000 American adults and found that more than half — 54% of them — feel like no one knows them well. The survey also revealed that 56% said the people they surround themselves with "are not necessarily with them," and about 40% said they lack companionship, meaningful relationships and that they feel isolated.

The Campaign to End Loneliness compiled some sobering statistics on how this lack of social interaction can cause serious health problems:

Loneliness, living alone and poor social connections are as bad for your health as smoking 15 cigarettes a day. (Holt-Lunstad, 2010)

Loneliness is worse for you than obesity. (Holt-Lunstad, 2010)

Loneliness

Loneliness is likely to increase your risk of death by 29% (Holt-Lunstad, 2015)

Lonely people are more likely to suffer from dementia, heart disease and depression. (Valtorta et al, 2016) (James et al, 2011) (Cacioppo et al, 2006)

The way I look at it because we are in a social media bubble where every image is filtered and cultivated to tell the world we have a perfect existence. By extension, everyone we're connected to feels they have to have a perfect existence, too. That creates a ripple effect. As a result, you don't often see someone being genuine and real. Then, if there is someone having a bad day, they might put in an 'unspoken prayer request' that gets out on social media, except it's not unspoken anymore once it's posted. People often won't say what it is they're upset about because they're afraid of saying their truth, and so they wind up getting a bunch of emojis and maybe a few comments of concern. What does that really solve? We don't fix problems by patting them on the head. You have to talk about it, peel the onion, and find out what layers are involved so you can solve these troubles.

I honestly believe this is a generational problem. We have decided everything is about us. Almost 40 years ago, the 'Me Generation' came up in the era of Ronald Reagan and the trickle-down economy. We were told we were selfish and had to become independent. Now the Millennials have come of age, and they were raised to be the most self-centered generation that ever lived — in large part because nobody has ever expected anything of them. *(Yes, I'm broadbrushing, and yes, there are those who do not fit this description.)* If you are part of Generation X, you know that you were expected to let yourself in the house after school, do your chores, your homework, and when your parents came home, if it wasn't done, there would be trouble. Now you have a generation whose expectation is they're going to do whatever they're going to do, and they're still going to be universally loved and coddled in that process. Because they've been told that the world revolves around them, being self-centered is an underestimation of what's really going on. The only thing they see in the world is themselves. They read an article, they see a news item, and immediately, everything is applicable just to them *(which is why I felt the need to include my disclaimer above!)*

Millennials are also the first generation whose entire lives have unfolded during the development of the online world. They've always known the Internet. Social media is a key part of their existence. They may understand the use of social media better than any generation alive, but I would like to suggest they are also more attached to social media than any other group.

The great irony of social media is you are bombarded by potentially billions of other people, and yet you are all by yourself.

Sheer Numbers Aren't Relationships

Marketers use the social media management platform Hootsuite to coordinate all their promotional efforts across sites like Facebook, Twitter, and Instagram. To help them with this effort, Hootsuite released some interesting data:

- There are 3.48 billion social media users in 2019, up 9% over the previous year.

- 3.26 billion people use social media on mobile devices, up 10% year-on-year

- There are 4.39 billion Internet users in 2019, up 9% since 2018

- There are 5.11 billion unique mobile users in the world today, up 2% from 2018.

It's dizzying to think there are that many people all engaged in the same activity together, at the same time, and yet we're all alone. Where I'm from, we call this a paradox.

Only on social media can you congregate with so many people yet still be completely isolated. This creates other tangled social problems, namely bad behavior, and poor manners. The relative anonymity of the Internet — and simply not being in the same physical space as other people — creates a sort of freedom that some people happily exploit to say things they would never dare speak in person. It's like people who make rude gestures and yell obnoxious comments at other drivers from inside their own car. They have the illusion of a protective, 2,000-pound bubble around them. Social media has made it far worse, just without the potential for fender-benders. There's still plenty of road rage online.

This presents a special challenge for people struggling to cope with the onslaught of information, comments, and distractions on social media.

When you think you are the only person in existence, of course, everything seems like a personal affront. By extension, there's a movement afoot that says you have to be the person who sees the wrong in all things in order to be the most righteous person in the room. Well, when that attitude gains traction, people don't talk to one another, and they stop being honest with each other. We really don't know who's who anymore. People are hiding their worst sides — but also their best sides — because they don't want to be criticized. We're no longer in a world that can take criticism or give criticism effectively.

Those Who Yell Loudest, Win

This is becoming a bigger and bigger concern. Look at our corporations. Time was, they would imagine and create new products and decide on the best way to get them to the public so the public could make a decision about whether to buy. Now those same corporations will change a marketing plan or a sales plan based on five angry online Twitter users who scream and call them names. That basically tells the public that opinions don't matter unless you are screaming about it online. It all starts to become a self-perpetuating and self-feeding machine — a real problem for all of us. If you're not a screamer, most likely, you'll just shut up. That's how people get marginalized, shoved aside. Screaming is not the answer, although social media enables the problem.

You can see this play out in the political arena. Most people who vote in a general election say they're choosing between the 'lesser of two evils.' You very rarely hear from somebody who goes to the polls because they're excited about their candidate.

To understand why this happens, we have to go back to the primary process where political

16

parties choose their candidate to run in the general election. Now, you have a very small percentage of voters who participate in the primaries. Most people don't think it matters when the reality is the primary matters more statistically — because you have fewer voters participating. Your vote actually counts more, and you're selecting amongst all your various types of candidates to see who's going to the general election. It's the one chance you'll get to pick somebody that you could get behind, someone for whom you could cheer! But people don't vote unless they feel they **have** to vote, and that usually means they wait until the general election. As a result, you have a very small group of people writing the first chapter of history because they're picking the candidate everyone else will evaluate in the general election.

People voting in the primaries are often voting with a vengeance. They may be those yellers and screamers. They pick the candidate **they** want, which is how you wind up with candidates in the general election that the majority of voters don't want, but are stuck with. By not voting in the primaries, you're letting the screamers dictate the outcome. Look at any primary — local, state, national primaries — to see how this plays out.

Something similar happens with modern dating, as people choose the ways in which they try to learn about each other. A large number of young people are dating later and later in life — or refusing to date because it doesn't look like it will have the 'right' outcome. They give up on the process. It's not just online dating sites that trigger this behavior, but also reality TV dating shows where people see an unnatural way of forming relationships.

They're choosing based on surface characteristics instead of discovering the really interesting things that make each human different.

When Isolation Leads to Despair

Older generations learned how to interact among groups of friends and with friends of friends. Younger people interact

more often by text, by social media, where they can cultivate the perfect version of themselves. If your entire universe thinks you're perfect, then of course, you don't want to be seen as anything less than perfect. So they don't date. They stop hanging out with other people. Somebody might find out they're not perfect. They may even actually believe they're perfect, and to maintain that illusion, they avoid real human interaction. That's an unsustainable way to live.

It leads to loneliness, which leads to depression. Now suicide rates are going through the roof because too many people think there's no way out of this trap. How can someone step out of their virtual-world comfort zone when it looks like everyone else is perfect, and they have it all figured out?

Today suicide is the 10th leading cause of death in the United States. An average of 129 people kill themselves every day, reports the American Foundation for Suicide Prevention. That's more than 47,000 lives lost every year. The suicide rate has increased every year in America since 2008. *(Scarier, this does not include suicide attempts)*. Hospitals report patient statistics to the CDC — the Centers for Disease Control and Prevention. In 2015, which is the most recent year for available numbers, approximately 575,000 people were treated in hospitals for injuries due to self-harm.

There is increasing evidence that the Internet and social media can influence suicide-related behavior, reports the U.S. National Library of Medicine. Cyberbullying is one factor. So is lower self-esteem triggered by prolonged exposure to social media. When we compare ourselves to the lives of others we see online, we may perceive something missing in our own lives — never knowing whether what we've seen from other people is true. For people at risk of self-harm, the Internet is a vast repository of chat rooms and message boards where anonymous strangers can and do discuss anything, including killing themselves.

An online phenomenon known as 'The Blue Whale Challenge' involves participants completing different tasks over a 50-day period with the final challenge being to kill themselves. This social network "game" has been documented in more than a dozen countries.

In Japan, suicide is the leading cause of death in men among the ages of 20-44, and for women 15 to 34. As I write this, Lithuania, Russia and South Korea have the highest rates of suicide on earth. In terms of total loss of life, India and China top the list because these are two of the most populous countries in the world.

In JAPAN suicide is the leading cause of death in men ages 20-44 and women 15-34

LITHUANIA, RUSSIA & SOUTH KOREA have the HIGHEST rates of suicide on EARTH

INDIA & CHINA have the highest loss of life from suicide due to being the most populous countries

It might surprise you to learn some of the *least technologically-developed* nations have the *lowest suicide rates.*

Data Source: https://afsp.org/about-suicide/suicide-statistics/ and
http://worldpopulationreview.com/countries/suicide-rate-by-country

As they take stock of their online lives, people are slowly starting to recognize this dead-end existence for what it is, but the question becomes: how do you break out of this cycle? How can we rejoin society and stop living the life of an off-the-grid hermit? It's a life out of balance. We need to restore equilibrium.

Yes, we enjoy the Internet. Myself, I enjoy being able to look at old television shows, being able to look up information at my fingertips, but I also still enjoy going to the library because I like the smell and feel of books. I'm afraid to lose that ability because libraries are closing and books are vanishing. If that happens, we'll be at the whim of people who police the Internet and decide what we read. You can see this happening on information sites like Wikipedia. Anyone can change the content of an article on Wikipedia to suit their own agenda. Sometimes it happens faster than the watchdog editors can react *(or perhaps, they choose when to react and when to sit back)*. Once again, you can't always be sure if what you're seeing online has any basis in reality.

Let's Get Real

So here we are. There's no getting back the time we frittered away yesterday on social media. You don't get to curate the past, but you can curate your own future. That's why we're *Peeling the Onion* — to live better lives.

People have disengaged from their own lives. I'm convinced it was an unintended consequence of social media. Facebook has the largest reach into the population, but what the creators did not anticipate is we would go in there believing we would find friends and colleagues, start liking and commenting on their posts, sending them a birthday message and such, but all we're doing is substituting that for actual interaction. We thought we would be more engaged with people, but we're actually less engaged because we're not trying to go further anymore, to go deeper. In the 15 years I've been on Facebook, I interact with my real-life circles less than I once did.

People get addicted to the notifications and the "likes," on social media because we feel good about it. That little "thumbs up" icon activates the dopamine center in our brains, but it's still just artificial interaction. It's time for a change. Best of all, there's no downside. A living, breathing world of real friendship and love is waiting, right where it's always been.

Ready? Let's get real.

Chapter 2.

So Where Do We Start?

Crawling out of our social media cave is just the beginning. Take a deep breath. Put down the phone. Okay. Let's go.

To know me, you'd think I would consider social media to be heaven-sent! As a child, all the way up until high school, I was ridiculously shy. Quiet. Withdrawn. I was the teacher's pet because of that *(well, and also being willing to stay in from recess to grade papers)*. I had a small circle of friends. Now, I still *knew* everybody. Luckily, one of the hallmarks of being shy is you never really go sideways with anyone. I was fortunate in that sense! By the end of college, I had made many more new friends, but lost track of quite a few from my hometown days. Then came the career. Busy, busy. Family. Even busier. A calendar just packed with things to be done. So it goes. You get me.

Probably like you, with the advent of social media I initially saw an opportunity to reconnect with people I hadn't seen or spoken to in years. Finding out where they are now in life was just fun! Logging into a site like Facebook is so fast. So easy. You can nibble on a piece of pound cake and find out whose dog just had puppies, then check out the political rantings of your crazy friend from college — all in a matter of minutes. Ha! If we only kept it to a few minutes, which we don't. Instead of really getting to know people, social media became a crutch. It became easier to look at the surface of many people rather than engaging with any of them in an individual, meaningful way.

Evidence: my high school class. We didn't even bother to have a 5-year reunion. We didn't have a 10-year reunion, either *(at least, I don't think so!)*. We tried to have a 20-year reunion, and there were maybe 22 people who showed up. It was still so much fun. We all knew roughly who each other was from 20 years ago (and through social media). That's 10% of the graduating class. That's less than half the average turnout for a 20-year reunion, according to Group Travel, an organization that tracks these sorts of statistics. For a 20-year high school reunion, it used to be that you could expect nearly 30 percent of the graduating class to show up. That was before social media. My guess is that it's declining rapidly as the years progress.

Psychology Today recently noted the value of attending reunions and, by extension, reconnecting with people in person. It's valuable because we usually *(keyword: usually)* develop wisdom and maturity as we age. "Encountering our former classmates and recalling old memories, good and bad, may help us gain better insight into who we are now and how we got here," say doctors Shoba Sreenivasan and Linda Weinberger. "The opportunity to engage in conversations that are not time restricted encourages deeper communication. Even mundane activities, like going for a walk or taking a long drive, can stimulate the friends to reminisce or discuss their feelings and thoughts beyond a superficial level."

Finding Substance Beyond The Shallow Waters

An amusing movie called *Romy and Michele's High School Reunion* came out in 1997. In it, two women decide to attend their 10-year reunion, and they make up all sorts of nonsense to impress their former classmates. Like, they claim to have invented Post-It notes. Today, that lie could be easily discovered by a simple Google search. Now people are less likely to tell

such tall tales at their reunion. Instead, they can (and do) create a beautiful, entirely fictional portrait of their lives and put it out there on social media, where their reality is not likely to be discovered, much less challenged.

The strange irony of social media is that platforms like Facebook can make it easier to find old friends and even plan reunions with them, but social media can also make people reluctant to attend a reunion. They might think they already know what everyone is up to — by reading social media posts. Of course, they're not getting the whole story.

There's another dimension to this. As we've seen, the loneliest people gravitate toward platforms like Facebook. People ages 25-34 — who right about now would be attending their first reunions — report on surveys that they're often lonely. Studies show that even daily Facebook connections don't replace the benefits of actual human contact.

At my reunion, we knew about some of our other classmates, the basics, the tidbits we had seen on social media, but nobody could tell you in-depth what somebody else had turned into or where they had gone with their life. That was an eye-opener for me. It's a generational thing. My dad still goes to his reunions. My grandmother always went to her reunions as long as she was alive because that was her big chance to reconnect with people.

Anyone Can Go Mining for Silver; You Gotta Dig Deeper for Gold

Shouldn't we work harder to learn about people? Shouldn't we spend time looking them in the eye and talking to them? When you only see people so often, yes, you have the crutch of social media where you can glance at their life day-to-day, but you actually know them less than you would if you just spent 20 minutes actually talking to them. Because talking, as opposed to the superficiality of social media, is when you start peeling the onion. You're listening to their words, and the inflection tells you what's behind the words, the eye contact that reveals so much, the body language that brings their words to life. That's communication.

So when somebody tells you, "I'm fine," if you were to read that in a social media post, you might move on because you think they actually are just fine. But when you're having that face to face conversation, you realize that you need to ask more questions based on the tone of their voice, their body language. Because you notice the fact that here's somebody sitting with you and they obviously haven't told you the whole story yet. They're working their way toward telling you that story, but they haven't gotten up the gumption to let it out. These are all little nuances that we're losing, but we can get them back.

As a personal test to myself, I decided I had to get these relationships back. So I'm trying to physically reconnect with

friends from the past, knowing that there's a special connection to people who knew you way back when. There's an old saying, "Make new friends, but keep the old; one is silver, the other is gold."

We have a mindset where we're only focused on silver, which we probably have more of, and not on gold.

Let's talk about that gold for a minute. One of my favorite reconnected moments involves a friend of mine from Governor's School, high school, and college. We were such good friends, and it continued through college, but we eventually went our own ways in life. We reconnected on social media, and I realized one day that I really missed talking to him because he's super smart — one of those few people with whom you can have intellectual conversations in serious depth. I adore those kinds of real conversations! He was in town, and I saw that on social media, so we went to lunch — and we ended up spending three hours talking. We talked about where we each had gone and what our lives looked like versus what we thought they were going to look like. We talked about so many different topics, and it was amazing. It's a different conversation on social media now that we spent three hours reconnecting, because I can hear his voice again when I read his words.

Some people will find it hard to pick up precisely where they left off. Maybe it was decades ago. That's okay. The important thing is to begin. To make the effort. Figure out where your starting point is so you can blend the two sides of your world. Maybe your way to begin is with a message or text to an old friend. I don't think any of us want to give up the benefits of social media or our technology, but we also don't want to let these things be the only connection that we have to other humans. For me, that first step is setting a personal goal to have face-to-face conversations.

What if you're not ready to see somebody you knew 20 years ago? My challenge to you is to begin peeling your own onion first. Ask yourself why you're not open to conversations because if you have changed over the years, you must understand that others have changed, too. Life comes at all of us from different directions. So the first step could be reading a social profile and deciding, hey, there's somebody you want to have a conversation with. Maybe you spot something online, like another human being who needs care and empathy. What if you just offered to be available to your friends? Let them know. Remind them, if necessary. Don't wait for someone else to reach out. That's what everybody else is doing. The initiative is yours.

Remember Pen & Paper?

I posted recently that I had the urge to write some happy notes. "Who needs a happy note?" I asked. I just put it out there to the random public. Well, I had over 70 people respond, "I need a happy note." And what's happened since then has been pretty intriguing. It took some time, and frankly, that's one of our challenges when we peel the onion: overcoming our excuse that we don't have the time to do it. The excuse for me not going to  lunch with my old friend would be, who has three hours to spend? Well, it wasn't three hours that I spent. I didn't look at it that way. Instead, it was three hours that I invested in him as a human and me as a human. That's how I looked at writing these notes. It was an investment of time. If you can possibly send a handwritten note on stationery, do it. This is an elegant and all-but-lost art. Writing by hand, almost always deepens your thoughts. It's special. Shows that you really care. Think about it. When was the last time you received a handwritten note in the mail? Exactly. Still, if you can't find a mailing address for a friend, an online post is better than not writing a note at all. It's really just a prelude to a deeper connection in-person, anyway.

Already, social media has changed how we communicate — mainly by making our conversations shallow and superficial. This leads to the impoverishment of language. People seldom use complete sentences when clicking away on their keyboards to post a message. Speed is the priority, so instead of agreeing in plain terms with someone, we type "k," and it's on to the next message. Gotta run? R U sure? K. TTYL.

This shorthand, along with the use of slang, is steadily ruining grammar and syntax for a generation. When this begins to creep into speech patterns, people start to sound like they're from another planet. Or maybe they just come across as ignorant. The real risk, though, is poor communication. People are also missing out on the unique beauty of language. There is music in the spoken word. Inspiration in the well-written thought.

Throughout history, the people we most admire and respect are individuals who express themselves clearly and with eloquence. People who know how to communicate, tend to be more successful because they are able to explain their ideas in a way that others can understand — even appreciate and endorse when the ideas are expressed effectively. Beyond connecting with people at a deeper level, good communication is also the only way you are going to get what you want out of life.

Social media is no substitute for a real social life. In truth, social media diminishes our communication skills and actively prevents us from interacting with other people in more meaningful ways.

As I'm writing these happy notes, I'm also reading all of my friends' timelines *(because we can't forget that Facebook et al only show us what they want to show us)*. If those friends don't always show up in your timeline, then what you don't see, you don't know. I found that some of the people I've known for a while have been through some really rough experiences recently, and I didn't know that. It doesn't make me a bad person for not knowing — it just means they were not on my radar. Well, suddenly, they were. In reading their posts, I was able to personalize the notes and send them out. The results have been pretty fascinating.

Some people haven't responded at all. Some people I suspect just want the attention — which they need for some personal reason — and that's as good a reason as any! But for other people, they said my note came on a day when they really needed it. I've got people opening up to me about things that they obviously need to talk about, but didn't have somebody they felt comfortable talking to. Well, I'm glad to be that person. You can be, too. Imagine a social life for yourself where you are making a difference in the lives of others, not just scrolling absentmindedly through selfies and random photos of what your acquaintances claim they had for lunch.

Social media communication just doesn't go much deeper than that. Pictures of the kids. The new puppy. A sunset snap taken during the beach vacation. With the widespread problem of hacking and data breaches, smart people are only going to reveal just so much personal information about their lives online. Friends aren't learning much about each other on social media, only the most basic superficialities. Is that enough? Not for me and, I suspect, not for you, either. We want more out of life.

The answer is to use social media as a catalyst for deepening the relationship, not as an excuse for it. So write a note and send it. That's the first step.

You can't tell me you're too busy to do that when the average time frittered away on social media is about two hours a day. When we're talking about interacting with people face-to-face versus online, it's the difference between passing the time and filling the time. The former has meaning. The latter, not so much.

Time to Dial Those Digits

Now you've written a personal note and established contact more substantive than an emoji. Next, make a phone call. I know that sounds precious, but this is what you must do. Pick up the phone. Smile and dial.

One of your excuses is probably going to be, "What if this person doesn't want to hear from me?" As good human beings, we give ourselves all of the negative pep talk we can possibly drum up. We get in our own way and don't make the phone call. But I'll challenge you with this: in the era of smartphones, the person on the other end has two options — decline or accept. If they don't want to talk to you, they'll hit decline. Then you'll have the beautiful opportunity to leave

a voice mail saying hello and telling the person you're thinking about them. That's it. That's your little script. Easy.

Still, effort is necessary. Risks are involved. There is the fear of rejection, which can be crippling for some.

I prefer to look at it another way, in a positive light. When you want to fix a beloved recipe, but you don't feel like peeling the onion because it might make you cry — goodness, it might even make your fingers smell terrible — well, you know what happens when you leave out the onion? Your recipe is not going to be the crowd-pleasing triumph it might have been. Peeling the onion is worth it.

What we're trying to accomplish is not necessarily hard, but it's going to take a little more effort. In truth, peeling the onion is probably easier than the *fear* of peeling the onion. And once you do take the time, you may be pleasantly surprised by how welcome your overture truly is for the recipient of your kindness. That's a win. For everyone involved.

Now let's go deeper.

The secret
of getting ahead
is getting started.

~ Mark Twain

Chapter 3.

Going One Level Deeper.

I realize that not everybody reading this book grew up in a Southern church. Maybe you'll wish you had if you realized how good we had it.

Church potlucks were magical! The entire congregation would get together for a meal every so often. Everyone brought a dish — nothing was store-bought. Somehow, we always ended up with the right assortment of entrees, vegetables, and desserts. You'd think sometimes we'd have nothing but cobbler or green bean casseroles, but that never happened. You made your specialty to bring, and dinner just figured itself out. You'd get a plate and sit down with people and eat. Does that seem unusual? I've been told that the church potluck is completely outside of the experience and comfort zone of many. This startling revelation got me to thinking.

Part of the reason we might not like eating with other people is the feeling of being trapped. You've got to think of something to say for an hour or more — and also be prepared to respond to what your neighbor is saying. The beauty of the church potluck was that you *knew* small talk would be involved, but you also already knew most everyone who'd be there. Even as a child, you'd learn quickly what would be acceptable as small talk — and what would not!

35

Peeling the onion begins with small talk. I don't know many people who are ready to sit down and dive immediately into a philosophical discussion of the meaning of life — or even their own lives — with strangers. You're supposed to work your way up to that!

Small talk does **not** start with politics. I'm still not sure how society devolved into a space where what happens in the privacy of the voting booth became the very first identifier used. Weather used to be a great small-talk topic, but now you even have to be careful when you're talking about the weather unless you want to get into a discussion about global warming, which can turn back around to politics pretty quickly. Sports also used to be easy until announcers started adding politics into their discussion of coaches and players, and don't get me started on what is happening to Title IX!

Anyhoo, before we get into the gentle art of small talk, let's consider the appropriate way to begin — with a greeting.

The Art of the Handshake

Shaking hands with friends and new acquaintances is the hallmark of civilized society. I'm an affectionate person, but I still want to caution that rushing in for a hug should be reserved for close friends who are expecting that level of contact, which should be based on past experience. That's just the world we live in today. Save the hugs for the close circle *(or for the people who "need" a hug, and you can read them if you'll pay attention)*.

Shaking hands is still on the front lines of polite society. It's so ingrained in our culture that few people might realize the practice dates to the 5th Century B.C. in ancient Greece. Warriors greeted each other with open hands to show they weren't holding weapons. Sounds like a reasonable approach if you're trying to make friends.

Don't worry about whether your offer to shake hands will be accepted. I'm telling you now: 99.99 percent of the time, it will. It's so deeply embedded in the social contract; almost no one wants to be known as the rude person who doesn't shake hands. *(Germophobes, I still love ya, but I also know full well that you have hand sanitizer in your purse, so you'll be okay!)*

When you shake hands, maintain eye contact, and say something, both sincere and pleasant. A simple "so good to see you" is sufficient. *Bonus tip: if you don't recall the name of the person whose hand you're reaching for, introduce them to someone nearby and let them pipe up with their name — it works most of the time!*

A firm handshake with a maximum three pumps is all you need. More than three is just odd — like you're engaging in some sort of secret society greeting ritual. Also, this is not a test of strength.

No need to crush someone's hand. *(And while we're on the topic, can you please start teaching your children how to shake a hand? They'll fare far better in Junior Achievement if they can express themselves in this way!)*

If you arrive before your friend at your meeting place, stand up when they arrive.

Above all, and I hate to be all "mama hen" here, but make sure your hands are clean and dry. If you're enjoying an iced tea, wipe the condensation off your palm with a napkin before shaking hands. Because otherwise, eew.

Small Talk: Opening the Floodgates to Deeper Conversations

The best part of the church potlucks was that everybody knew each other, making small talk easy. In that era, all of our time was spent together in community. You generally went to work and to school with the same people *(and their cousins, neighbors, ex-wives)*. Potluck suppers encouraged everyone to slow down, enjoy themselves, get to know each other better, and eat without fear of calories or recrimination. In fact, not eating dessert was liable to get you in trouble!

You must be a master of small talk to succeed in face-to-face meetings, cocktail parties, dinner hours.

Every topic is its own onion that can go deeper and deeper. But first, I want to stress that there are three topical areas not suitable for Level 1 conversations: politics, religion, and relationships. Starting off with one of these topics is not peeling the onion, it's more like chopping the onion. Save those heavy subjects for a time when you've already gone several layers deeper. Your friends will let you know when they're ready. People drop hints when they're talking, whether they intend to or not. Asking follow-up questions always demonstrates that you are listening. Just be careful that your questions don't suddenly chop the onion in half.

I mention this also because we cannot predict where a conversation is headed. If it runs off the rails, you need to be ready to make a course correction. If small talk veers in an awkward direction, you must act quickly to redirect the conversation. Be sincere, yes, but you must likewise learn to be smooth. This is important because we cannot begin to peel the onion if we become alienated from the person to whom we're talking. Here are some strategies and techniques that work for me when I need to take the wheel.

Redirect

If the conversation lurches into territory that makes you or your friend squirm *(DANGER, WILL ROBINSON!)*, simply say that there are many possible viewpoints, but it's not your area of expertise. This is a polite acknowledgment of an issue without taking a position, especially with politics and religion. It also shows that you are listening. Now redirect! Ask your friend about the best thing she's done recently, perhaps something that made her smile in the last week. Most reasonable people will take the hint and change course with you.

Try Icebreakers

Peeling the onion always begins with the outer layer. Start the conversation — or steer it in another direction — with any of these surefire icebreakers that get people talking:

- The weather *(if you're a fun sort, use the WTForecast app to make weather hilarious!)*

- Favorite sports teams

- Sharing which Netflix series is your current binge

- Popular restaurants

- Read any good books lately?

- Vacation recommendations

- Any new movies that you can suggest?

Give a Compliment

Everyone likes compliments. One of the easiest ways to change a conversation that's moving in a negative direction is to praise the other person's knowledge of the subject without necessarily endorsing their position. Then you can ask how their viewpoint affects their situation. Say your friend is on a rant about a crumbling relationship. You could praise her awareness of the problem as the first step either to fixing it or moving on with life. That moves the conversation deeper. That's peeling the onion.

Switch Gears

Conversations are a two-way street. If your companion is droning on and on without pausing so you can respond, listen closely for keywords that might provide an opening to change the subject to a more meaningful conversation that involves both of you. If you've been listening to a 15-minute complaint about the heat, smile and say you'll both probably be complaining about the cold come January, "speaking of which, do you have any good ideas to keep kids entertained during the holiday break?"

Change the Subject Immediately

Some topics are off-limits. It doesn't matter how deeply you've peeled the onion. Only you can decide which ones are taboo, but you probably already know them. Some people are loathe ever to discuss their sex lives, while others can't stop talking about it. If a subject comes up, that's on your forbidden list, change the subject then and there. Make a nice comment about your friend's appearance. Ask where she bought that darling purse or those cute shoes. If they still can't take the hint...

Be Direct

If you've tried to change the subject and it's just not working, you are completely within your right to say, "This is something I don't feel comfortable talking about," or, "I really don't feel like I know enough about this to discuss it." Then immediately offer an alternative topic. Because peeling the onion involves sharing, there may come a time when off-limits topics become fair game.

There's no need for this to occur until all participants in the conversation make it clear they are ready.

When All Else Fails, Excuse Yourself

Take a bathroom break. Take a deep breath. This gives you a chance to consider some other topics to discuss. Even if a conversation becomes painful — perhaps especially if it becomes painful — taking a short break will allow you to salvage the time invested. We know that peeling the onion is desirable. Valuable. So is our time! If I know anything to a certainty, it is that time is our most precious resource. Life is fleeting. The number of hours ahead remains unknown to us all. Health, wealth, these benefits mean nothing without time. Make the most of it by giving and receiving value from every conversation.

Maintaining Eye Contact

Looking someone directly in the eyes during a conversation is the single best thing you can do to make a connection with another

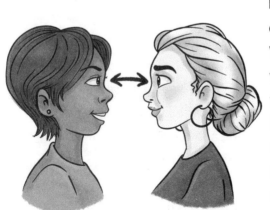

human being outside of the spoken word. With eye contact, we communicate with one another on both conscious and unconscious levels. Locking eyes can communicate many things, which is why we use words to clarify and explain ourselves. Eye contact is an entirely voluntary movement that originates in the cerebellum of the brain. You can improve eye contact with practice.

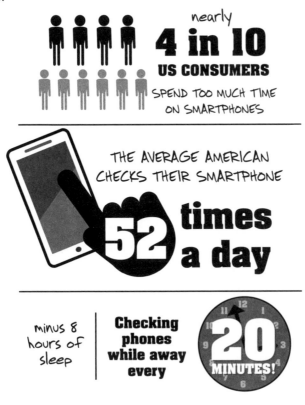

First, we have to put down our phones. Nearly 4 in 10 U.S. consumers say they spend too much time on their smartphones, according to a study by Deloitte, the professional services network. Americans check their smartphones an average of 52 times a day. Assuming most of these people sleep at least 8 hours a day, that means while awake, they're checking their phones at least every 20 minutes. That's just the average — and to be honest, I think it's waaaay lower than reality!

When you glance at your screen, your focus is broken, and the person you're with gets the message that the phone is more important than they are. You may have just lost that connection.

Scientific studies have also shown that one consequence of living on social media is that we don't use the cerebellum enough to track three-dimensional space. This includes making eye contact with other people. The cerebellum (Latin for "little brain") is that part of our noggins in the back of the head that manages motor control, attention, and our ability to process language. Staring too much at a screen literally causes this part of our brain to stagnate from disuse. The cerebellum begins to atrophy and does not function at peak performance. As a result, it becomes harder to make and maintain eye contact and to focus on what the other person is saying. See? Putting down the smartphone turns out to be the smart move. Want proof? Ask yourself if you can recite your very first phone number-and if you can currently recite your best friend's number. Once upon a time, we could learn these things and retain the information because we had better focus.

That focus can really be demonstrated when you learn to maintain eye contact, not falling prey to the temptation to look over the shoulder of your colleague in order to see who's coming next. Those in leadership positions, or who are seeking to improve their own status, can be the worst offenders of this — and boy howdy, people notice!

There is a challenge to overcome with sustained eye contact: putting people at ease when they are not accustomed to someone looking them in the eye. Some of my younger friends, who devote much of their lives to staring at phone screens, tell me that it's "creepy" when I make prolonged eye contact with them. Entire generations are growing up in a world where they spend time with their peers, but no one is looking at each other. They're all sitting in a circle, engaged with their smartphones, and responding to each other in monosyllables.

I tell these friends that eye contact is proof that I'm listening. That I care. This usually puts them at ease. Once they understand a new sensation, it's no longer awkward. The other benefit of maintaining eye contact is it becomes very difficult for your mind to wander while you are this engaged in communicating with someone. You can remain focused.

Eye contact is a very intimate form of communication. When you look someone in the eye, you can really learn a lot about what they're thinking. To get better at eye contact, you must open yourself up to intimacy again. Let me be clear: this is not about sex. This is about deepening the relationship below the next level. People often live their lives right below the surface, but just barely below that surface is everything else that's going on. You never know when it's going to emerge.

What if we all started carrying a handkerchief again? There's a lot to be said for the person who's open to an emotional conversation and also has a comforting solution at hand. When the tears begin to fall, what a quiet comfort it is to have someone pass you a Kleenex! My father-in-law always has a handkerchief handy — and the kids really do notice that he's at the ready when they need it.

Why not practice with somebody you love? Start by having a random conversation with no screens. Try phone stacking. This is standard practice when I meet friends for lunch. Everyone puts their phones in a pile. First person who reaches for their phone gets the penalty, which usually means picking up the entire restaurant check. I can tell you my belief (and experience) that when picking up the check is at stake, my friends and I have much livelier conversations. For the duration of lunch, you'd best believe that our phones stay parked in the middle of the table like a pile of bricks at a construction site!

By applying these skills in a sincere and compassionate manner, you can begin to express more true feelings — concern, empathy, real emotion. I'm not talking about therapy-level stuff, mind you, but just honest conversation where the real you comes through. You laugh more freely, and you don't feel the need to flee from the room when you say something in error. Instead, it turns into an "inside joke" between you and your friend. Suddenly, life just gets better.

Now that we've got the conversation going let's lower our defenses and be open with each other in the way only genuinely real people can. It's a great feeling.

Chapter 4.

Sharing the Things Not Everyone Knows.

There are stories you would never post on Facebook. Would you ever share about that time you got fired from a job for your own mistakes, even if it was yesterday? *(Especially if it was yesterday?)* What about those "one that got away" love stories? How many of your friends know about that pair of crazy aunts who turn every family reunion upside-down, dumping a bucket of stress on everyone? When was the last time you saw someone on social media own their failures?

These stories are (usually) reserved for the people with whom you spend the most time. They're shared over personal dinners, whether at a restaurant or at home. Maybe you'll hear them while attending a baseball game, which lasts hours or avoiding the Macarena at your cousin's third wedding. Certainly, you learn things while traveling with other people when they are most relaxed and more inclined to lower their guard.

When I mention these types of stories and who we share them with, in your mind, I'm betting you've already reduced your possible audience down to single digits (the well-known and documented Circle of Trust). The good news is, you know that the people on that shortlist will also reciprocate by sharing their stories. How do we reach a place where we're comfortable sharing with more people beyond that short list? Are we ready to listen to that someone who really needs to talk — and for whom the Circle of Trust is perhaps nonexistent? If we can peel the onion with more people, the better all our lives can be.

Still, when the sharing gets really personal, it's going to get harder. You have to be willing to become vulnerable. With sharing, just like the onion, it's not the outer layer that makes you cry. Only when you've peeled down to the really good and flavorful parts are you liable to cry, either from happiness or in sorrow or in angst. That's a risk that comes with its own reward — deeper, more meaningful relationships.

The problem is, we're living in a world of curated perfection. Flaws and feelings get swept under the rug so that only the surface remains. The desire to curate an idealized faux-reality stems from the complete lack of control over ourselves that existed in the pre-digital world.

The price we pay for the ease of social media is our perception of its permanence. There is the sense that if we post something, it had better be perfect because it's going to be forever. We all know that mantra, 'Twitter is Forever,' and kids know that they'll be judged at the age of 30 by what they said at the age of 11. The idea of permanence makes some people reluctant to share more of their lives online beyond the nice snapshot of the crème brûlée they ordered for dessert. As we know from experience, online conversation tends to stick to the shallow waters where it's safer.

Ask yourself why you, yourself, are so willing to jump on a political candidate for something she said, or for an acquaintance he made, for a policy belief that has changed, without allowance for the passage of time? It seems that many of us expect to receive a grace that we are not offering to others.

We're also seeing more troubling news about the risk of announcing too much of your personal life on social media. Facebook has acquired a reputation as a sloppy custodian of our data. One security breach exposed the personal information of 50 million users. In another incident, contact information and other private data was stolen from 14 million Facebook users.

The company itself was hit with a $5 billion fine by the Federal Trade Commission for the misuse of users' data acquired from Facebook by Cambridge Analytica, a big-data company designed to influence elections around the world. Cambridge Analytica has since shut down, while Facebook continues to thrive by matching users with advertising, based on everything we share. Let me be clear. We *are not* Facebook's customers. We are the product Facebook sells to advertisers. Facebook likes to promote the fact that it's free "and always will be," but we pay a hidden price for giving away our information online. The real cost of that has yet to be determined.

Is it any wonder some people limit their social media activity to posting pictures of what the new puppy did today? Meanwhile, our children just toss up mainly pictures of themselves and each other. Glowing, perfectly composed photos with pretty frames and cute filters.

In a way, I feel sorry for my kids. They are less likely to look back at their high school yearbook and question their hair choices, their fashion choices. When I was in high school, we didn't have the ability to look at 200 digital photos of ourselves to pick the best one — because yes, there *was* a right and a wrong way to wear that teased hair with the 'claw' bangs. You were at the mercy of the school photographer *(and if you're not following @ awkwardfamiliyphotos on Instagram, correct that immediately!)*.

My kids are growing up in a world where we take a family picture, and they immediately want to look at what was taken to approve or disapprove, then take and retake until a photo is deemed perfect. Remember this, though — when you look at your photos 10 years from now, you're not going to be looking for perfection. You'll be looking at the <u>people</u> in the picture with you. We need to get back to a place where it's okay to shake your head at your own poor choices, even laugh about them *(those '80s bangs, natch)*.

It's okay to say, "I don't want to be that version of myself anymore. I want to grow and change."

The permanence of social media has the unintended consequence of making people think they can't change, but we all do. The beauty of being human is you go through different things in life.

You deal with aging parents. You have children with medical issues, or maybe you can't have children. You're married or wish you were married. You're divorced or wish you were divorced. All of those things continually shape you, like what the ocean does to glass. There are people who collect sea glass precisely because it has been polished to a beautiful, glossy sheen. The edges that would have cut you are now gone. They've been polished to a marvelous rounding that has a special texture and a feel — like a touchstone you keep in your pocket to rub for security.

We're making a mistake if we let social media convince us that people can't be polished and transformed by the lives they lead.

That's why I worry my kids will be painted forever as the people they were at 14. In life, you try on different versions of yourself to see which is the best "You" then it starts to cultivate and evolve over time. When we're so focused on social perfection right now, and the idea that everything is permanent, we easily forget there are moments in life that connect us to other people.

Teenagers no longer go walking around the mall, mixing and matching with other social groups. Instead, they create group texts which can cut someone out of the conversation without even the courtesy of acknowledging the old "silent treatment." *(As an aside, the original* Parent Trap *with Hayley Mills illustrates this point and remains essential viewing in my house — NOT the remake!).* I encourage parents when they get together with friends and their kids, to set a "no screens" rule. In this way, kids learn how to chat with their peers, which is a valuable experience — especially when it's not their usual group of friends.

Sharing Life's Most Difficult Moments

Only recently did I learn that an acquaintance had lost her husband of 47 years. A mutual friend had thought to share this with me. "Is she okay?" I asked.

"No, she's not okay," came the response.

Life as she'd known it had completely and utterly changed.

When you think about someone's life-changing irrevocably and forever, you realize that's something we almost never discuss. We don't have honest conversations with each other about how it's okay to grieve for an extended period of time. We're living in a society that says: 'suck it up and keep going, no matter what!'. Well, there are times when some people just can't keep going. If they can't talk about it and be honest, then how can we expect them to push through? For me, learning that a friend is not okay means I need to do a better job of reaching out. When I look at her social profiles, it seems like everything is okay. What if you buffer that online stalking with a real phone call, to then discover that indeed, there's a lot more going on. We have to do a better job of asking those questions, of peeling the onion. It means that moment by moment you let other people see your frailties. This is the magic sauce for allowing others to share theirs.

It's easier to help other people when you've been helped. How willing are **you** to accept the help of other people? We are so independent nowadays that we often have trouble accepting help. Now flip that coin over — if you're the one offering to help and it's rejected, it's hard as a giver to keep offering!

Pause and look at what's happening in somebody else's life. Look at their social profile — look for clues. Photos are a good start! If someone is posting photos without their spouse, ask if everything is all right *(note: this is NOT the time to suggest that your perennially single brother is available)*. If you notice something, just make yourself available. It's not about prodding or being a busybody. Gently reaching out is about allowing that person to talk. If they shut you down? Change gears! At least you've been bold enough to plant a seed. Not everybody is comfortable with having an intense conversation with you. That's when you should send a note. There's a lost art in the handwritten note when people open the mailbox and see they've gotten something that's not a solicitation or a bill.

If a note doesn't seem like the best solution, food might be the answer. Where I grew up, the admission ticket to the church was (and still is) a 9 x 13 casserole dish. If a conversation is not on the table, food always is! Now, don't worry about getting in your own way, fretting about whether someone is on a gluten-free diet or has some other food restriction you don't know about. This is where the gift is in the giving. Just be sure to explain what is in the lovely dish you've prepared for them and leave it at that. If they receive your food and can't eat it, well then, they're going to throw it away, but they're not going to tell you about it. That's okay, too.

The point is, the very act of preparing food is its own reward that will give you the satisfaction that comes from kindness and basic human compassion. When I have stopped what I'm doing in order to bake a bereavement cake, it allows me to think about someone else — to consider their life and what I might be able to contribute, however modest, to make their life just a little better. This puts my focus on something far more meaningful than a Facebook post. (*Bonus tip: if you're a terrible cook, ignore this whole section.)

Of course, when you are a giver, there are limits to everything. You do have to balance your energy. You have a finite amount of energy, and, yes, there are people who exist to suck the life right out of you if you let them. If somebody's going down that road, you need to be strong enough to say to them, "I think you need a professional relationship." Direct them to a support group. Suggest a therapist. Steer them toward those resources because you're not a

Caveat: When you're thinking about sharing the raw parts of your life, you have to make sure you're balancing those conversations with other experiences. If you become that person who only talks about drama, the issues you're having, you will turn people off. Make sure you're balancing your sharing with positive aspects of your life. Make inquiries about other people. You don't want to give anyone social exhaustion. However, if you have something you want people to know, lay it out there with an honest request for their input.

licensed therapist. There's a lost art in listening to one another, but it doesn't mean that you have to get abused by being willing to do so. Know your limits. Over time, you may be pleasantly surprised to discover that your boundaries and tolerance actually become greater.

By peeling the onion, we uncover new joy in our own lives through a deeper understanding of those we care for. The equilibrium of this give-and-take is the hallmark of a beautiful friendship — and the focus of our final chapter.

**A faithful friend
is a strong defense;
And he that hath found him
hath found a treasure.**

~ Louisa May Alcott

Chapter 5.

If You Have More Than One Good Friend, You Have More Than Your Share.

Once upon a time, in those dark days before the Internet took hold of our collective consciousness, there was a British anthropologist named Robin Dunbar, a renowned specialist in the behavior of primates. During his research in the 1990s, Dr. Dunbar discovered an interesting correlation between the brain size of primates and the average size of their social groups. He then made some calculations using human brain size and came up with a provocative proposal: people have the cognitive ability to maintain up to 150 relationships with other individuals. That's the magic number. The good news is, it means we can have more friends than a baboon, but maintaining a quantity of friendships like bees in a hive or ants on a hill, well, that's just out of the question. Our minds max out at 150. Sure, we all know or have known more than 150 people, but at any given point in our lives, we can sustain active, functioning relationships with no more than 150.

Now, if you have 3,000 connections on Facebook, I'm not suggesting that you need to unfriend 2,850 of them. The point is simply that, unless you're superhuman, you're not going to be able to manage more than 150 relationships with other people. As for genuinely close friendships, I'm inclined to believe that this number will be significantly smaller.

Dunbar's discovery was based on his observations that when social groups become larger than the members can mentally handle, more restrictive rules and laws will need to be put in place to maintain the stability of the social group. Otherwise, there will be chaos. This is why we trust our closest friends implicitly, while people outside our social circles *(or even at the outer edges)* might be considered sketchy until proven innocent. Trust is a hard commodity to come by these days. It is earned. It is also a two-way street that gets paved only by practice.

We can't really trust someone we don't know, so we built societies with laws and rules. And because our brains are not wired to maintain stable relationships with more than 150 folks at a time, we had better cherish the ones closest to our hearts.

Yet people still want 10,000 followers on Twitter. They want to max out their Facebook friends, get all the followers on Instagram that they can, to scale up.

When you look at Dunbar's small number, you're really considering your most meaningful human relationships. We're not talking about the thousands of Facebook friends you've never met and likely never will.

Dunbar's number includes the people you know well enough that you would willingly go out to dinner with them. You know whether they're caring for aging parents. You know what their kids' flaws are. The reason we're limited to 150 is because you and I have a finite amount of energy, and you can't be invested in everybody you've ever met. That's a job for God — trust me, He can handle things you and I just can't!

It's not realistic to manage a thousand relationships. It would completely wear you out on other humans, and when you're burned out on other humans then it's harder to like them. It's harder to talk to them. When it's harder to talk to them, it's harder to have a meaningful relationship — which is why we wind up with 5,000 friends on Facebook, where we can click *like-like-like* and feel like we've done our job.

To avoid burnout and that cycle of pain, we're going to think about this in terms of those top 150 relationships we can nurture. Those 150 people are your trusted core — that Circle of Trust. Most people have a small handful of friends who know everything about them. In fact, they're so close to you they don't go to the funeral with you when your mama dies because they're sitting at your house. Somebody has to stay at the house, to be ready to receive people after the funeral, and they know you well enough that they don't have to physically be at the funeral because they can do other things for you. That's a really special gift. There's so much truth in the adage: 'If you have one good friend, you have more than your share.'

Shine Your Diamonds

That one best friend — that one special relationship — is a jewel. I'm not sure that we place a high enough value on those anymore in a world where we call each other "bae" — and "BFF" is so superficial. We run the risk of forgetting that that *best friend* is the one for whom you will drop everything you are doing and run to them because they need you. It doesn't matter why they need you — when your special person calls, off you run!

Out of your 150 potential, manageable relationships, you'll think about those five people who you really love and trust. Maybe it's just one.

So my question is, what are you doing for those people that makes them feel like they're one of those top five? Do you share meals with them? Do you visit them? Do you invest in life with them?

One of my best friends in the world, he moved away several years ago for his job. He and his beloved broke up. Then he fell in love again — and I haven't even met his new love IRL! Doing friendship virtually is just HARD. The one thing that really ties us together, and has for over 20 years, is our personal book club. If I read something amazing, I will mail the book to him. He mails books to me. I might get a box from my Robert with four books in it, and y'all — that's better than Christmas! He marks each book with the date he read it, which makes me feel like I'm right there with him. That's not something you can do for a thousand people. That's something you do just for your very best people. He's also the person for whom I will *always* take a call. On the night when I lost an election primary in my first bid for public office, it was his call that I took. This is how you know your top 5 people. You don't want to talk to everybody else, but you *need* to talk to them.

We have to get back to this kind of life. Back to the relationships with people who don't care about your politics or with whom you're sleeping. They don't care if your kids have done something horrendous — failed a class, skipped town on the back of a Harley, whatever. They love you for who you are: for your flaws, your positives, and everything else. For whatever reason, you landed in life together.

Sometimes We Turn Down the Wrong Road

Why are we putting those special relationships to the side to manage 5,000 fake people online? This is where we have to fix our priorities. Let's turn around. Get your kicks on Route 66. We should be looking for the scenic route, not the shortcuts of the social media interstate that deliver thousands of people to our Facebook page almost as fast as we can click.

Now think for a moment: Who's your best friend? Does this wonderful person date back to grade school? These are the friendships that seem to survive anything. Like they say, a cockroach will be able to survive a nuclear war — and your closest friendships will endure whatever life throws their way and yours.

Best friends have that indefinable "click" with you. They have been there in good times and bad, and everything in-between. They know your parents and your siblings, and you know theirs.

The thing is, with the greatest friendships, like that sweet inner core of an onion, you don't get to the goodness immediately. You have to peel it back layer by layer. We must take the risk of crying and the pungent smell that won't come off our hands. The sweet is never as sweet without the sour. But think about the alternative: shallow interactions that are utterly dependent on a reliable Internet connection or generous data plan *(which also assumes we remembered to charge the smartphone overnight)*.

Here's the hard question: Are you still nurturing that friend you've known forever, or have you let her slip away, where you no longer know the details of her life?

"Yes," I hear you say. "It happens. But we're all so busy. Life is hard."

Life is indeed hard. So hard that, in truth, we should put this in perspective.

Life by the Numbers

Statistics from the U.S. Government's annual mortality report show the average lifespan in America now stands at 78 years, 7 months and 6 days *(the government rounds it off to 78.6 years, but I say make every day count, so let's count every day)*. As we saw in Chapter 1, the average time spent on social media is about 2 hours a day. Now let's say a person starts exploring the world of social media at age 13 and keeps at it for the average life expectancy. Subtracting the first 13 years before our young friend hopped online, that's a lifetime of 65 years, 7 months and 6 days for those who are keeping count. If we stick to the average daily engagement of two hours on social media, our friend from the time she's 13 until her dying day will invest a solid 5 and a half years of her life just on social media. Five and a half years. Staring at a screen.

From 2003 to 2018, the average daily amount of time Americans spent reading for personal interest fell by six minutes to less than 16 minutes a day, according to the American Academy of Arts and Sciences. Not surprisingly, during that same period, time spent online and watching television only increased.

Another fun fact: the average American will invest 13 solid years plus two months at work. The Bureau of Labor Statistics tells us most people will change jobs nearly a dozen times over a lifetime, but the time commitment is still 13 long years. That's almost 114,000 hours of life spent at work.

This brings us to the real perspective. How much time will people spend socializing in-person with their friends over the course of a lifetime? Just 328 days. That's right. Less than a year. That's less than 1 percent of the average person's entire lifespan. *(Feeling guilty yet?)*

A study published in the Journal of Social and Personal Relationships found that it takes about 50 hours of time with someone before you will consider them a casual friend. That

average lifespan in America **78.6**	lifespan from age 13 to 78.6 **68 years, 7 months, 6 days**

2hrs average hours on social media daily	**5.5 YEARS** spent on social media in average lifespan	**13+ YEARS** spent at work (114,000 HOURS)

ONLY 328 DAYS SOCIALIZING WITH FRIENDS!
LESS THAN 1% OF THE AVERAGE LIFESPAN

almost doubles to 90 hours before you become real friends, and more than doubles again to about 200 hours before you would consider the person a close friend. That's the average time commitment. (*Results may vary.)

As for myself, I'm still trying to wrap my mind around the idea that someone would spend five and a half, full years of life clicking and swiping on a screen, but less than 11 months in the company of real friends. Now, I'm sure nobody wakes up one fine morning and thinks, "Hey, I do believe I'm going to spend five and a half years of my entire existence tootling around on Instagram." At least, I hope not!

We don't think in those terms. The world keeps spinning whether or not we're not paying attention. Time fades away. It's always flowing into the future even when we're not focused on the passage of time. Especially when we're not focused. That's how time slips through our fingers. *(Insert Jim Croce or Steve Miller song here!)*

Data Source: www.humanitiesindicators.org/content/indicatordoc.aspx?i=11094

Bring it on Home

The other day I was driving to an appointment, and a song by the great Ray Charles came on the radio. The song gave me pause. Perhaps you've heard it:

Come on, baby, let's have some fun

YOU ONLY LIVE ONCE
– AND WHEN YOU'RE DEAD, YOU'RE DONE

So let the good times roll.

You only live once is the key line to remember. Might as well chase our dreams, be good to others, and strive to make the world a better place. I've run for public office twice *(as of this publication date)*, and *(spoiler alert)* lost twice. This leads to two questions from pretty much everyone I meet: 'WHY did you run for office?' and 'Will you run again?' I'll tell you that I decided to run because I believed *(and still do)* that more of us than not want a better future — one with leaders who are vulnerable and transparent, who have grown and changed with time, and who are open to peeling the onion in ways that can benefit us all. I love asking questions and having discussions, which lead us to a place of understanding — even if agreement is not a part of that understanding. If you only live once, and if you believe something needs to change, then why not take a big leap of faith and see what happens? I'll never regret putting myself into the public arena because if you take no risks, there can assuredly be no rewards!

We owe it to each other to bring back those good times. We owe it to ourselves to go deeper than what we see on our screens.

We can do this. It's going to take some effort, maybe rearranging priorities and letting go of a few time-wasting habits. Simply the desire to do so puts us halfway on the path toward success. When we make an honest effort, the right people take note, and they embrace what we offer. While we have time on this earth, we have a choice. Let the good times roll.

When I think of people I've known and loved, friends and family who have meant so much to me and improved my life in so many ways, it's hard even now to accept that some of them are gone, and I will not soon see them again. I try not to dwell on the simple truth that my earthly time with them has ended. Instead, I feel great joy for having known them at all and that we invested precious hours together. I feel this because I know nothing lasts forever, least of all our fragile existence. We still have freedom to choose how we use our time, the most valuable commodity any of us will ever possess, never knowing how much time might be remaining to us. We can decide what we do with our lives and when and where and how we get it all done. I say connecting in person in real-time with real people is — and will always remain — on the shortlist of beautiful ways to enjoy life to the fullest as we learn from each other, giving and receiving the nurturing power of love, of genuine caring. If we are not here to help one another, how much meaning can life really hold?

Still, peeling the onion requires work. It involves crying and taking chances and being vulnerable. Yes, but the rewards are endless. To connect with another person sincerely, openly, without pretense or agenda. That is the goal. There is the promise of sweet goodness when we get to the center of that onion. An abiding satisfaction. If that's not enough, I always remember this: the sweet scent softens a harsh reminder of the fleeting hours ahead.

ABOUT THE AUTHOR:

Many know Leigh Brown for her accomplishments as a highly successful REALTOR® and a best-selling author. This just begins to scratch the surface. She is an award-winning educator and influencer. She is an innovative CEO and a must-see keynote speaker. In fact, she has spoken all over the world — from Garden City to Phnom Penh! She actively educates professionals in every realm of business leadership and relationships. Leigh is a do-it-all professional.

Leigh has a passion for motivating those around her to want more. She has worked with all ranges of the professional spectrum — from new-to-the-trade rookies to CEOs of massively successful brands. It is her ability to articulate complex concepts in ways that everyone can relate to that makes her leadership so impactful.

Leigh wants to leave her mark on the next generation of professionals. Whatever your field of business is, Leigh has tools that can promote growth and a team-oriented environment. She has the sales techniques; she has the experience; she has the PASSION! Leigh wants to help YOU!

Leigh lives in Charlotte, North Carolina with her husband, Steve, and their two children, Cora and Timmy.

Peeling the Onion is Leigh's third book. Her best-selling books, *The Seven Deadly Sins of Sales*™ and *Outrageous Authenticity,*™ can also be purchased in print or Audible on Amazon or by visiting **www.LeighBrown.com**.

 /LeighBrownSpeaker

 /LeighBrownSpeaker

 /LeighThomasBrown

 /LeighThomasBrown

 LeighBrown.com

Podcast: Crazy Sh*t In Real Estate
www.CrazyShitInRealEstate.com
Or search "Leigh Brown" on your
favorite podcast app

ABOUT THE ILLUSTRATOR:

Zoe specializes in character development for companies geared towards children as well as picture book illustration. She enjoys creating whimsical characters and loves to infuse her work with humor. Currently, Zoe runs an independent graphic design and illustration studio in Belmont, North Carolina (just outside of Charlotte).

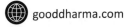 gooddharma.com

 /zoeranucci

CAN'T GET ENOUGH OF LEIGH BROWN?
THERE'S SO MUCH MORE!

REAL ESTATE • PERSONALITY • SPEAKER

Leigh is a dynamic public speaker, a motivating personal coach, a knowledgeable instructor, and a professional consultant. Book Leigh Brown today! **www.LeighBrown.com**

LEIGHBROWN
— & ASSOCIATES —
#MoreThanHouses

Over Leigh's years as a REALTOR,® she has lived out her motto of #MoreThanHouses — even before we had hashtags! She strives to make her community a better place through personal interactions and positive relationships on a daily basis. She has over 20 years of real estate experience, selling over 3,000 properties! Her understanding and knowledge of the greater Charlotte, NC area, Leigh is second to none. **www.LeighSells.com**

With the 2020 launch of One Community Real Estate,™ Leigh continues her mission to support and develop REALTORS® who are both leaders and advocates in their own communities while still striving to serve buyers and sellers as their REALTOR® advocate. **www.OneCommunity.RealEstate**

This comprehensive online course covers the growth path that Leigh herself followed to build a powerful and highly profitable brand. **www.LeighBrownU.com**

Crazy Sh*t in Real Estate! — a podcast that will shatter the HGTV-induced veneer of real estate, and celebrate the challenges of working in this wild, wacky business. **www.CrazyShitInRealEstate.com**

"...the best weapon in your sales arsenal is not all that fluff & puff. It's telling the truth." ~ Leigh Brown

The Seven Deadly Sins of Sales™ and *Outrageous Authenticity,*™ can be purchased in print or Audible on Amazon or by visiting **www.LeighBrown.com**.

NOTES

NOTES

NOTES

NOTES

NOTES

NOTES

NOTES

NOTES

NOTES

NOTES